SEVEN AMAZING

CONTINENTS

WORLD GEOGRAPHY & SOCIAL STUDIES

The Creative Research Handbook for Library & Internet Based Learning
Fun-Schooling With Thinking Tree Books

The Thinking Tree Publishing Company LLC

TABLE OF CONTENTS

flip to the back of the book for a list of "wonders" on each continent

ACTION STEPS

1. Go the library or bookstore. Bring home a stack of at least seven interesting books. Try and find one for each continent.
2. Choose music from all around the world to listen to when you study each continent. There is an album that accompanies this book.
3. Search for websites that have information about the continents as well as the world.
4. Choose books and websites that have lots of pictures and details.

MY WORLD WONDER WEBSITES

Leave space for 4 websites to be written in.

1. _____

2. _____

3. _____

4. _____

GO TO THE LIBRARY AND CHOOSE SEVEN BOOKS

1. Write down the titles on each book cover below.

_____

_____

_____

_____

_____

_____

_____

2. Keep your stack of books in a sale place so you can read a few pages from your books daily.

3. At the bottom, write down the websites you are allowed to use for research.

4. If you need more space for books, flip to the back of the book for more book pages. Have seven empty books in this spot.

SUPPLIES NEEDED

Pencils, Colored Pencils & Gel Pens

Africa

Africa

What do you know about it?

How big is it: _____

How many countries does it have: _____

Which oceans surround it: _____

Population: _____

Find and color the continent on the world map

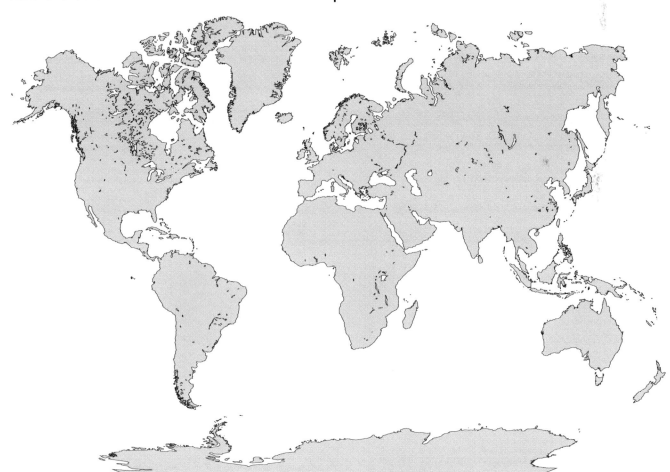

WORLD WONDER SEARCH

Name of Wonder: _____

Name the country: _____

List 5 interesting facts:

    1. _____

    2. _____

    3. _____

    4. _____

    5. _____

Illustrate it:

Africa

WORLD WONDER SEARCH

Name of Wonder: _____

Name the country: _____

List 5 interesting facts:

1. _____

2. _____

3. _____

4. _____

5. _____

Illustrate it:

Africa

WORLD WONDER SEARCH

Name of Wonder: _____

Name the country: _____

List 5 interesting facts:

1. _____

2. _____

3. _____

4. _____

5. _____

Illustrate it:

Africa

WORLD WONDER SEARCH

Name of Wonder: _____

Name the country: _____

List 5 interesting facts:

1. _____

2. _____

3. _____

4. _____

5. _____

Illustrate it:

Africa

WORLD WONDER SEARCH

Name of Wonder: _____

Name the country: _____

List 5 interesting facts:

1. _____
2. _____
3. _____
4. _____
5. _____

Illustrate it:

COLOR THE ANIMALS OF AFRICA

LIST 14 ANIMALS FROM AFRICA

Write them

1. _____

2. _____

3. _____

4. _____

5. _____

6. _____

7. _____

8. _____

9. _____

10. _____

11. _____

12. _____

13. _____

14. _____

Draw them

COUNTRIES IN AFRICA

Which countries do you know in Africa? Write them down:

1. _____	20. _____	39. _____
2. _____	21. _____	40. _____
3. _____	22. _____	41. _____
4. _____	23. _____	42. _____
5. _____	24. _____	43. _____
6. _____	25. _____	44. _____
7. _____	26. _____	45. _____
8. _____	27. _____	46. _____
9. _____	28. _____	47. _____
10. _____	29. _____	48. _____
11. _____	30. _____	49. _____
12. _____	31. _____	50. _____
13. _____	32. _____	51. _____
14. _____	33. _____	52. _____
15. _____	34. _____	53. _____
16. _____	35. _____	54. _____
17. _____	36. _____	55. _____
18. _____	37. _____	
19. _____	38. _____	

Show the countries on the map, writing the corresponding numbers

TRAVEL DREAMS

Where in Africa would you like to go?

_____

_____

_____

Why do you want to go here?

_____

_____

_____

What is the climate like?

_____

_____

_____

A unique fact:

_____

_____

_____

Illustrate something about this place

Africa

MOVIE TIME

Watch a movie or documentary about Africa.

Title _____

Rating:

Draw Your Favorite Scenes:

DRAWING TIME

Copy an illustration from one of your books.

READING TIME

Today's Date _____

_____

Book Title _____

_____

Write about what you are reading.

Draw about what you are reading.

STORY WRITING TIME

TITLE

_____

Names & Descriptions of Characters

_____
_____
_____
_____
_____

Share Your Story

_____
_____
_____
_____
_____
_____
_____
_____
_____
_____
_____
_____
_____
_____
_____

MUSIC OF THE WORLD

Listen to traditional music that represents this continent.
Try to find three different songs.

Name of Song _____
Country _____

Name of Song _____
Country _____

Name of Song _____
Country _____

What instruments are used?

_____
_____
_____

What do you like about the songs you listened to?

_____
_____
_____
_____
_____
_____

FILL THIS SPACE WITH YOUR FAVORITE THINGS ABOUT AFRICA

Asia

Asia

Asia

What do you know about it?

How big is it: _____

How many countries does it have: _____

Which oceans surround it: _____

Population: _____

Find and color the continent on the world map

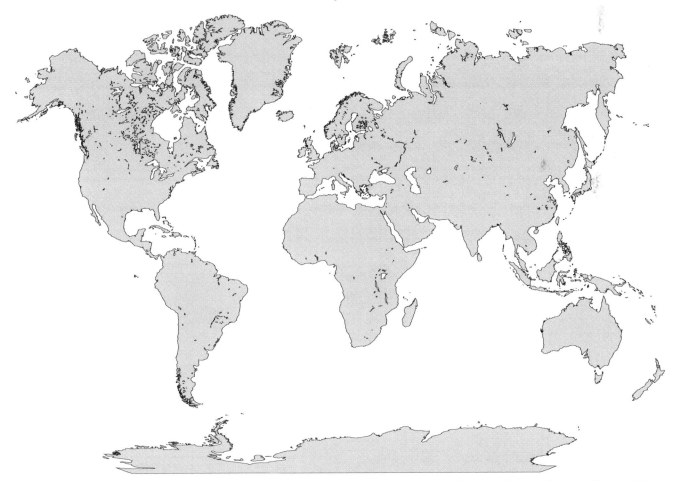

Asia

WORLD WONDER SEARCH

Name of Wonder: _____

Name the country: _____

List 5 interesting facts:

1. _____
2. _____
3. _____
4. _____
5. _____

Illustrate it:

Asia

WORLD WONDER SEARCH

Name of Wonder: _____

Name the country: _____

List 5 interesting facts:

1. _____

2. _____

3. _____

4. _____

5. _____

Illustrate it:

WORLD WONDER SEARCH

Name of Wonder: _____

Name the country: _____

List 5 interesting facts:

1. _____

2. _____

3. _____

4. _____

5. _____

Illustrate it:

Asia

WORLD WONDER SEARCH

Name of Wonder: _____

Name the country: _____

List 5 interesting facts:

1. _____

2. _____

3. _____

4. _____

5. _____

Illustrate it:

Asia

WORLD WONDER SEARCH

Name of Wonder: _____

Name the country: _____

List 5 interesting facts:

1. _____
2. _____
3. _____
4. _____
5. _____

Illustrate it:

COLOR THE ANIMALS OF ASIA

LIST 14 ANIMALS FROM ASIA

Write them

1. _____
2. _____
3. _____
4. _____
5. _____
6. _____
7. _____

8. _____
9. _____
10. _____
11. _____
12. _____
13. _____
14. _____

Draw them

COUNTRIES IN ASIA

Which countries do you know in Asia? Write them down:

1. _____
2. _____
3. _____
4. _____
5. _____
6. _____
7. _____
8. _____
9. _____
10. _____
11. _____
12. _____
13. _____
14. _____
15. _____
16. _____
17. _____
18. _____
19. _____

20. _____
21. _____
22. _____
23. _____
24. _____
25. _____
26. _____
27. _____
28. _____
29. _____
30. _____
31. _____
32. _____
33. _____
34. _____
35. _____
36. _____
37. _____
38. _____

39. _____
40. _____
41. _____
42. _____
43. _____
44. _____
45. _____
46. _____
47. _____
48. _____
49. _____
50. _____
51. _____
52. _____
53. _____
54. _____
55. _____
56. _____
57. _____

Show the countries on the map, writing the corresponding numbers

TRAVEL DREAMS

Africa

Where in Asia would you like to go?

_____

_____

_____

Why do you want to go here?

_____

_____

_____

What is the climate like?

_____

_____

_____

A unique fact:

_____

_____

_____

Illustrate something about this place

Africa

MOVIE TIME

Watch a movie or documentary about Asia.

Title _____

Rating:

Draw Your Favorite Scenes:

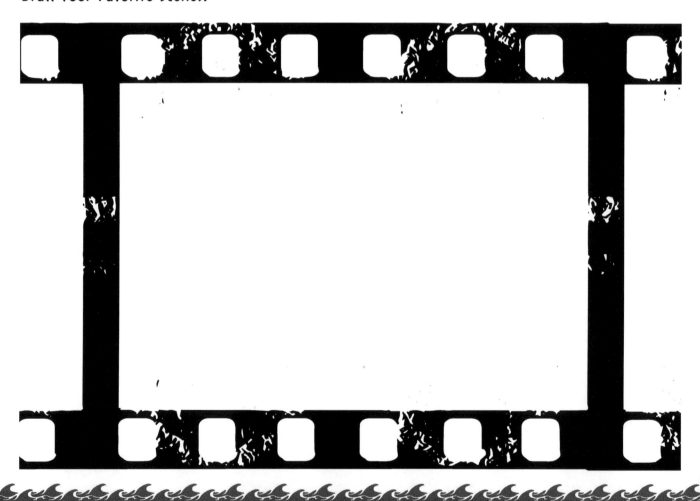

DRAWING TIME

Copy an illustration from one of your books.

READING TIME

Today's Date _____

Book Title _____

Write about what you are reading.

Draw about what you are reading.

STORY WRITING TIME

TITLE

_____

Names & Descriptions of Characters

_____
_____
_____
_____

Share Your Story

_____
_____
_____
_____
_____
_____
_____
_____
_____
_____
_____
_____
_____
_____

Asia

MUSIC OF THE WORLD

Listen to traditional music that represents this continent.
Try to find three different songs.

Name of Song _____
Country _____

Name of Song _____
Country _____

Name of Song _____
Country _____

What instruments are used?

_____
_____

What do you like about the songs you listened to?

_____
_____
_____
_____
_____
_____

FILL THIS SPACE WITH YOUR FAVORITE THINGS ABOUT ASIA

Europe

Europe

Europe

What do you know about it?

How big is it: _____

How many countries does it have: _____

Which oceans surround it: _____

Population: _____

Find and color the continent on the world map

Europe

WORLD WONDER SEARCH

Name of Wonder: _____

Name the country: _____

List 5 interesting facts:

1. _____

2. _____

3. _____

4. _____

5. _____

Illustrate it:

Europe

WORLD WONDER SEARCH

Name of Wonder: _____

Name the country: _____

List 5 interesting facts:

1. _____

2. _____

3. _____

4. _____

5. _____

Illustrate it:

WORLD WONDER SEARCH

Name of Wonder: _____

Name the country: _____

List 5 interesting facts:

1. _____

2. _____

3. _____

4. _____

5. _____

Illustrate it:

Europe

WORLD WONDER SEARCH

Name of Wonder: _____

Name the country: _____

List 5 interesting facts:

1. _____
2. _____
3. _____
4. _____
5. _____

Illustrate it:

WORLD WONDER SEARCH

Name of Wonder: _____

Name the country: _____

List 5 interesting facts:

1. _____
2. _____
3. _____
4. _____
5. _____

Illustrate it:

Europe

COLOR THE ANIMALS OF EUROPE

LIST 10 ANIMALS FROM EUROPE

Write them

1. _____
2. _____
3. _____
4. _____
5. _____
6. _____
7. _____

8. _____
9. _____
10. _____
11. _____
12. _____
13. _____
14. _____

Draw them

COUNTRIES IN EUROPE

Which countries do you know in Europe? Write them down:

1. _____
2. _____
3. _____
4. _____
5. _____
6. _____
7. _____
8. _____
9. _____
10. _____
11. _____
12. _____
13. _____
14. _____
15. _____
16. _____
17. _____
18. _____
19. _____

20. _____
21. _____
22. _____
23. _____
24. _____
25. _____
26. _____
27. _____
28. _____
29. _____
30. _____
31. _____
32. _____
33. _____
34. _____
35. _____
36. _____
37. _____
38. _____

39. _____
40. _____
41. _____
42. _____
43. _____
44. _____
45. _____
46. _____
47. _____
48. _____
49. _____
50. _____

Show the countries on the map, writing the corresponding numbers

Europe

TRAVEL DREAMS

Where in Europe would you like to go?

_____

_____

_____

Why do you want to go here?

_____

_____

_____

What is the climate like?

_____

_____

_____

A unique fact:

_____

_____

_____

Illustrate something about this place

Europe

MOVIE TIME

Watch a movie or documentary about Europe.

Title _____

Rating:

Draw Your Favorite Scenes:

DRAWING TIME

Copy an illustration from one of your books.

READING TIME

Today's Date _____

_____

Book Title _____

_____

Write about what you are reading.

Draw about what you are reading.

STORY WRITING TIME

TITLE

_____

Names & Descriptions of Characters

_____

_____

_____

_____

Share Your Story

_____

_____

_____

_____

_____

_____

_____

_____

_____

_____

_____

_____

_____

_____

MUSIC OF THE WORLD

Listen to traditional music that represents this continent.
Try to find three different songs.

Name of Song _____
Country _____

Name of Song _____
Country _____

Name of Song _____
Country _____

What instruments are used?

_____
_____

What do you like about the songs you listened to?

_____
_____
_____
_____
_____
_____

FILL THIS SPACE WITH YOUR FAVORITE THINGS ABOUT EUROPE

North America

North America

What do you know about it?

How big is it: _____

How many countries does it have: _____

Which oceans surround it: _____

Population: _____

Find and color the continent on the world map

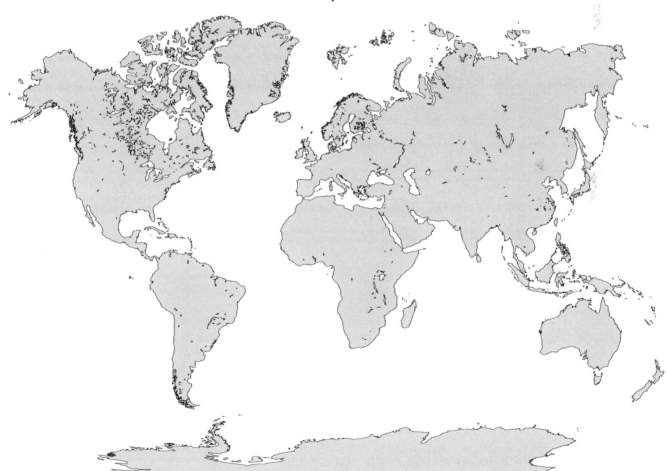

WORLD WONDER SEARCH

Name of Wonder: _____

Name the country: _____

List 5 interesting facts:

1. _____

2. _____

3. _____

4. _____

5. _____

Illustrate it:

North America

WORLD WONDER SEARCH

Name of Wonder: _____

Name the country: _____

List 5 interesting facts:

1. _____
2. _____
3. _____
4. _____
5. _____

Illustrate it:

North America

WORLD WONDER SEARCH

Name of Wonder: _____

Name the country: _____

List 5 interesting facts:

1. _____
2. _____
3. _____
4. _____
5. _____

Illustrate it:

North America

WORLD WONDER SEARCH

Name of Wonder: _____

Name the country: _____

List 5 interesting facts:

1. _____

2. _____

3. _____

4. _____

5. _____

Illustrate it:

North America

WORLD WONDER SEARCH

Name of Wonder: _____

Name the country: _____

List 5 interesting facts:

1. _____
2. _____
3. _____
4. _____
5. _____

Illustrate it:

COLOR THE ANIMALS OF NORTH AMERICA

LIST 14 ANIMALS FROM NORTH AMERICA

Write them

1. _____
2. _____
3. _____
4. _____
5. _____
6. _____
7. _____
8. _____
9. _____
10. _____
11. _____
12. _____
13. _____
14. _____

Draw them

COUNTRIES IN NORTH AMERICA

Which countries do you know in North America? Write them down:

1. _____
2. _____
3. _____
4. _____
5. _____
6. _____
7. _____
8. _____
9. _____
10. _____
11. _____
12. _____
13. _____
14. _____
15. _____
16. _____
17. _____
18. _____
19. _____

20. _____
21. _____
22. _____
23. _____

Show countries on the map, writing the corresponding numbers

TRAVEL DREAMS

Where in North America would you like to go?

_____

_____

_____

Why do you want to go here?

_____

_____

_____

What is the climate like?

_____

_____

_____

A unique fact:

_____

_____

_____

Illustrate something about this place

North America

MOVIE TIME

Watch a movie or documentary about North America.

Title _____

Rating:

Draw Your Favorite Scenes:

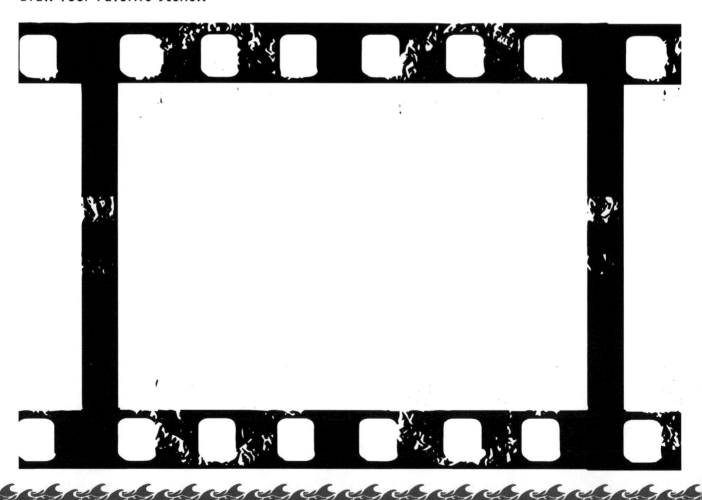

DRAWING TIME

Copy an illustration from one of your books.

READING TIME

Today's Date _____

_____

Book Title _____

_____

Write about what you are reading.

Draw about what you are reading.

STORY WRITING TIME

TITLE

_____

Names & Descriptions of Characters

_____

_____

_____

_____

Share Your Story

_____

_____

_____

_____

_____

_____

_____

_____

_____

_____

_____

_____

_____

_____

MUSIC OF THE WORLD

Listen to traditional music that represents this continent.
Try to find three different songs.

Name of Song _____

Country _____

Name of Song _____

Country _____

Name of Song _____

Country _____

What instruments are used?

_____
_____
_____

What do you like about the songs you listened to?

_____
_____
_____
_____
_____
_____

FILL THIS SPACE WITH YOUR FAVORITE THINGS ABOUT NORTH AMERICA

_____

_____

_____

_____

_____

_____

_____

South America

South America

South America

What do you know about it?

How big is it: _____

How many countries does it have: _____

Which oceans surround it: _____

Population: _____

Find and color the continent on the world map

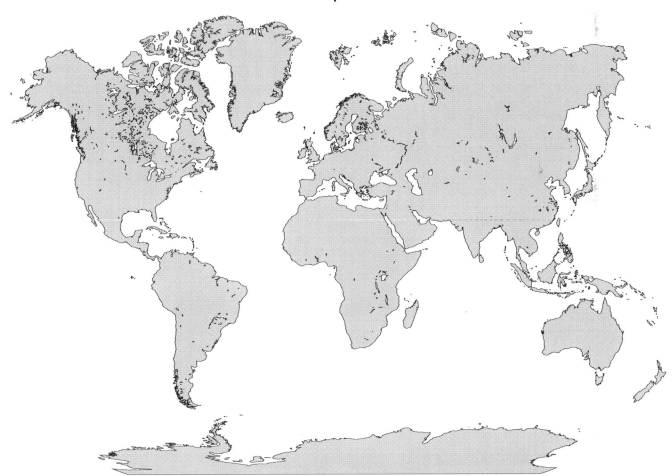

South America

WORLD WONDER SEARCH

Name of Wonder: _____

Name the country: _____

List 5 interesting facts:

1. _____
2. _____
3. _____
4. _____
5. _____

Illustrate it:

South America

WORLD WONDER SEARCH

Name of Wonder: _____

Name the country: _____

List 5 interesting facts:

1. _____

2. _____

3. _____

4. _____

5. _____

Illustrate it:

South America

WORLD WONDER SEARCH

Name of Wonder: _____

Name the country: _____

List 5 interesting facts:

    1. _____

    2. _____

    3. _____

    4. _____

    5. _____

Illustrate it:

South America

WORLD WONDER SEARCH

Name of Wonder: _____

Name the country: _____

List 5 interesting facts:

1. _____

2. _____

3. _____

4. _____

5. _____

Illustrate it:

WORLD WONDER SEARCH

Name of Wonder: _____

Name the country: _____

List 5 interesting facts:

1. _____

2. _____

3. _____

4. _____

5. _____

Illustrate it:

COLOR THE ANIMALS OF SOUTH AMERICA

LIST 14 ANIMALS FROM SOUTH AMERICA

Write them

1. _____
2. _____
3. _____
4. _____
5. _____
6. _____
7. _____

8. _____
9. _____
10. _____
11. _____
12. _____
13. _____
14. _____

Draw them

COUNTRIES IN SOUTH AMERICA

Which countries do you know in South America? Write them down:

1. _____
2. _____
3. _____
4. _____
5. _____
6. _____
7. _____
8. _____
9. _____
10. _____
11. _____
12. _____
13. _____
14. _____
15. _____

Show countries on the map, writing the corresponding numbers

South America

TRAVEL DREAMS

Where in South America would you like to go?

_____

_____

_____

Why do you want to go here?

_____

_____

_____

What is the climate like?

_____

_____

_____

A unique fact:

_____

_____

_____

Illustrate something about this place

South America

MOVIE TIME

Watch a movie or documentary about South America.

Title _____

Rating:

Draw Your Favorite Scenes:

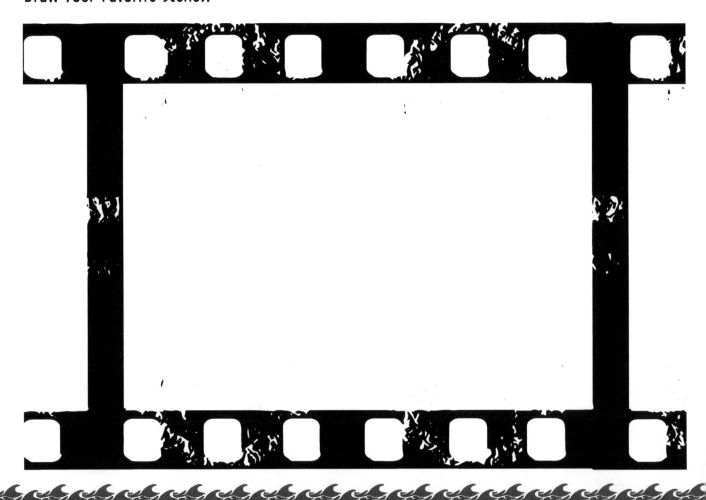

DRAWING TIME

Copy an illustration from one of your books.

READING TIME

Today's Date _____

_____

Book Title _____

_____

Write about what you are reading.

Draw about what you are reading.

STORY WRITING TIME

TITLE

_____

Names & Descriptions of Characters

_____

_____

_____

_____

Share Your Story

_____

_____

_____

_____

_____

_____

_____

_____

_____

_____

_____

_____

_____

_____

South America

MUSIC OF THE WORLD

Listen to traditional music that represents this continent.
Try to find three different songs.

Name of Song _____
Country _____

Name of Song _____
Country _____

Name of Song _____
Country _____

What instruments are used?

_____
_____
_____

What do you like about the songs you listened to?

_____
_____
_____
_____
_____
_____
_____

FILL THIS SPACE WITH YOUR FAVORITE THINGS ABOUT SOUTH AMERICA

Australia

Australia

What do you know about it?

How big is it: _____

How many countries does it have: _____

Which oceans surround it: _____

Population: _____

Find and color the continent on the world map

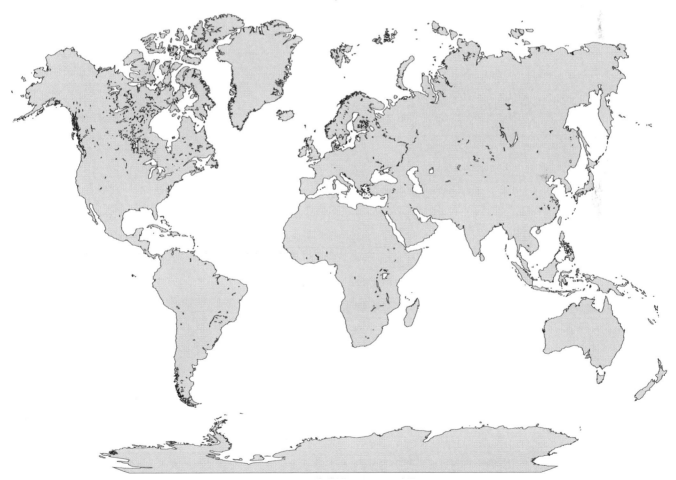

WORLD WONDER SEARCH

Name of Wonder: _____

Name the country: _____

List 5 interesting facts:

    1. _____

    2. _____

    3. _____

    4. _____

    5. _____

Illustrate it:

WORLD WONDER SEARCH

Name of Wonder: _____

Name the country: _____

List 5 interesting facts:

1. _____

2. _____

3. _____

4. _____

5. _____

Illustrate it:

Australia

WORLD WONDER SEARCH

Name of Wonder: _____

Name the country: _____

List 5 interesting facts:

1. _____
2. _____
3. _____
4. _____
5. _____

Illustrate it:

Australia

WORLD WONDER SEARCH

Name of Wonder: _____

Name the country: _____

List 5 interesting facts:

1. _____

2. _____

3. _____

4. _____

5. _____

Illustrate it:

Australia

WORLD WONDER SEARCH

Name of Wonder: _____

Name the country: _____

List 5 interesting facts:

1. _____
2. _____
3. _____
4. _____
5. _____

Illustrate it:

COLOR THE ANIMALS OF AUSTRALIA

LIST 14 ANIMALS FROM AUSTRALIA

Write them

1. _____
2. _____
3. _____
4. _____
5. _____
6. _____
7. _____

8. _____
9. _____
10. _____
11. _____
12. _____
13. _____
14. _____

Draw them

PROVINCES OF AUSTRALIA

Which provinces do you know in Australia? Write them down:

1. _____

2. _____

3. _____

4. _____

5. _____

6. _____

7. _____

Show the provinces on the map, writing the corresponding numbers

TRAVEL DREAMS

Australia

Where in Australia would you like to go?

_____

_____

_____

Why do you want to go here?

_____

_____

_____

What is the climate like?

_____

_____

_____

A unique fact:

_____

_____

_____

Illustrate something about this place

MOVIE TIME

Watch a movie or documentary about Australia.

Title _____

Rating:

Draw Your Favorite Scenes:

DRAWING TIME

Copy an illustration from one of your books.

READING TIME

Today's Date _____
_____

Book Title _____
_____

Write about what you are reading.

Draw about what you are reading.

STORY WRITING TIME

TITLE

_____

Names & Descriptions of Characters

_____

_____

_____

_____

Share Your Story

_____

_____

_____

_____

_____

_____

_____

_____

_____

_____

_____

_____

_____

MUSIC OF THE WORLD

Listen to traditional music that represents this continent.
Try to find three different songs.

Name of Song _____

Country _____

Name of Song _____

Country _____

Name of Song _____

Country _____

What instruments are used?

_____

_____

_____

What do you like about the songs you listened to?

_____

_____

_____

_____

_____

_____

FILL THIS SPACE WITH YOUR FAVORITE THINGS ABOUT AUSTRALIA

Antarctica

Antarctica

Antarctica

What do you know about it?

How big is it: _____

How many countries does it have: _____

Which oceans surround it: _____

Population: _____

Find and color the continent on the world map

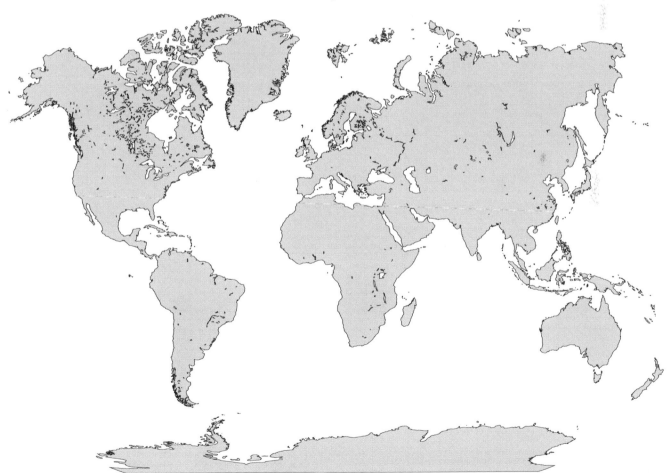

WORLD WONDER SEARCH

Name of Wonder: _____

Name the country: _____

List 5 interesting facts:

1. _____

2. _____

3. _____

4. _____

5. _____

Illustrate it:

Antarctica

WORLD WONDER SEARCH

Name of Wonder: _____

Name the country: _____

List 5 interesting facts:

1. _____

2. _____

3. _____

4. _____

5. _____

Illustrate it:

Antarctica

WORLD WONDER SEARCH

Name of Wonder: _____

Name the country: _____

List 5 interesting facts:

1. _____

2. _____

3. _____

4. _____

5. _____

Illustrate it:

Antarctica

WORLD WONDER SEARCH

Name of Wonder: _____

Name the country: _____

List 5 interesting facts:

    1. _____

    2. _____

    3. _____

    4. _____

    5. _____

Illustrate it:

Antarctica

WORLD WONDER SEARCH

Name of Wonder: _____

Name the country: _____

List 5 interesting facts:

1. _____

2. _____

3. _____

4. _____

5. _____

Illustrate it:

COLOR THE ANIMALS OF ANTARCTICA

LIST 14 ANIMALS FROM ANTARCTICA

Write them

1. _____
2. _____
3. _____
4. _____
5. _____
6. _____
7. _____

8. _____
9. _____
10. _____
11. _____
12. _____
13. _____
14. _____

Draw them

Antarctica

TERRITORIAL CLAIMS OF ANTARCTICA

Which territories do you know in Antarctica? Write them down:

1. _____

2. _____

3. _____

4. _____

5. _____

6. _____

7. _____

8. _____

9. _____

10. _____

Show the territories on the map, writing the corresponding numbers

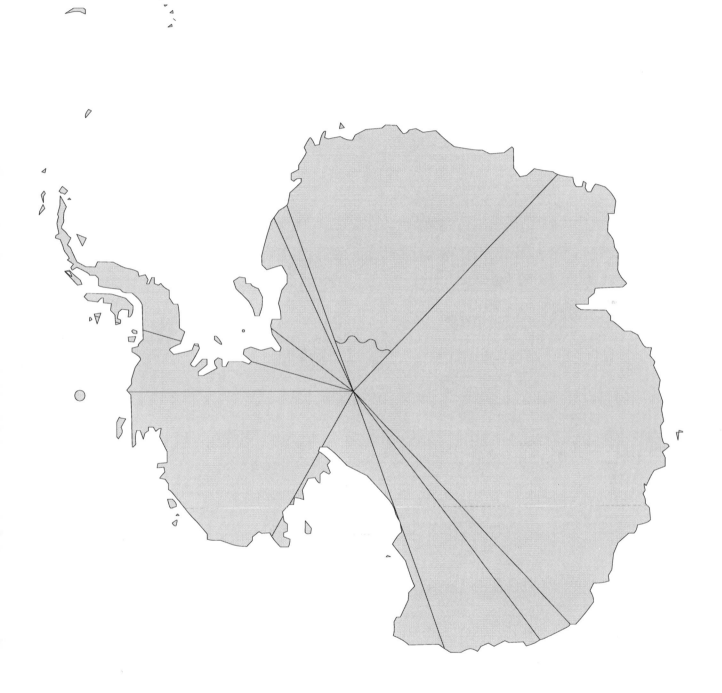

Antarctica

TRAVEL DREAMS

Where in Antarctica would you like to go?

_____

_____

_____

Why do you want to go here?

_____

_____

_____

What is the climate like?

_____

_____

_____

A unique fact:

_____

_____

_____

Illustrate something about this place

MOVIE TIME

Watch a movie or documentary about Antarctica.

Title _____

Rating:

Draw Your Favorite Scenes:

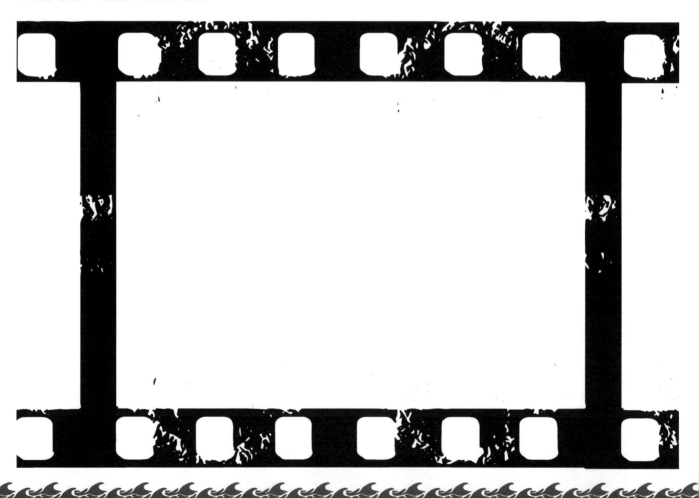

DRAWING TIME

Copy an illustration from one of your books.

READING TIME

Today's Date _____

_____

Book Title _____

_____

Write about what you are reading.

Draw about what you are reading.

STORY WRITING TIME

TITLE

_____

Names & Descriptions of Characters

_____
_____
_____
_____

Share Your Story

_____
_____
_____
_____
_____
_____
_____
_____
_____
_____
_____
_____

Antarctica

MUSIC OF THE WORLD

Listen to traditional music that represents this continent.
Try to find three different songs.

Name of Song _____
Country _____

Name of Song _____
Country _____

Name of Song _____
Country _____

What instruments are used?

_____
_____
_____

What do you like about the songs you listened to?

_____
_____
_____
_____
_____
_____

FILL THIS SPACE WITH YOUR FAVOURITE THINGS ABOUT ANTARCTICA

World Wonder Search

AFRICA
1. Mkambati Nature Reserve
2. Mount Kilimanjaro
3. Thunderstorm in the Savannah
4. Namib Desert
5. Oasis in the Idehan Ubari Sand Sea

ASIA
1. Batu Ferringhi Beach
2. Ban Gioc Detian Falls
3. Leye-Fengshan Geopark
4. Ghaghara River
5. Yading Natural Reserve

EUROPE
1. Grosse Scheidegg
2. Volga river
3. Krka Waterfalls
4. Bialowieza Forest
5. Egremni beach Island

NORTH AMERICA
1. Monument Valley
2. Cibola National Forest
3. Athabasca Falls
4. Pukaskwa National Park
5. Otter Cove in Acadia National Park

SOUTH AMERICA
1. Kukenan-Tepui
2. Seashore of Columbia
3. Victoria Amazonica
4. Andean Altiplano
5. Los Glaciares National Park

AUSTRALIA
1. Lucky Bay Cape
2. Blue Mountains
3. Devil's Marbles
4. Lake Argule
5. The Nambung Pinnacles

Copyright

Made in the USA
Las Vegas, NV
04 February 2023

66922267R00096